I0060114

A Fiscal Ode

By John Thomas 2nd

Nyota Nyeusi
Washington, DC

Copyright © 2016 by John H. Thomas 2nd

All rights reserved. No portion of this text may be reproduced in any manner or by any means without the express written permission of the copyright owner.

ISBN-13: 978-0-9979889-0-1
ISBN-10: 0-9979889-0-8

Once upon a time, in the land of the Dutch,
    there arose commodities priced at far too much.

And what was most shocking about their economic power
    was that these market marvels were no more flowers.

See, Turkish tulips were an instant sensation,
    but after their arrival came a viral mutation.

As a result, their pedals looked to be in flames,
    and this special array induced prices to go insane.

Of course, this sounds foolish, but we must understand
  it was simply all a matter of supply and demand.

These tulips, which were coveted as status symbols for the wealthy,
  took years to cultivate and much care to keep healthy.

So, with limited numbers and many wanting to buy them,
 it was inevitable that eventually they'd be highly priced items.

But, costs kept increasing, sometimes many fold,
 and it quickly became clear the market needed to be controlled.

The Dutch saw this and tried to ban investment shorts,
       however, this threat would need more effort to abort,
for the elevating value would just keep on rising higher
       and was only made worse by a growth in French buyers.

Unsurprisingly, with this rapid price inflation,
       the nation soon was flooded with investor speculation.

Even normal tulips, therefore, gained a cost increase,
  which naturally made trade no easier to police.

A nascent futures market had chance to, hence, expand
  to the point where the products rarely would change hands.

And as the tulip sales became more abstract
    the more fallacy one witnessed in contracts.

Deals were, thus, made often with little thought
    about the true intrinsic value what was being bought.

Indeed, at one point tulips became such a rage,
    just one could cost ten times a craftsman's yearly wage.

Eventually, though, such optimism proved rash
    as this awesome market boom became an awful market crash.

It started one day when an auction was called,
      but no buyers attended and the hosts were appalled.

The panic then spread and unbelievably
      a collapse began unfolding immediately.

Sellers couldn't sell nor could debtors pay their debts.
They had taken tremendous gambles but couldn't cover their bets.

How silly they all felt as the market evaporated
and they fully analyzed what had them so captivated.

Before they couldn't see it because of pride and greed,
    but the flower they exalted was as useless as a weed.

With no production purpose or capacity for service,
    this plant that they all loved was basically really worthless.

11

The moral of the story is never just trust the crowd,
        though they act extremely confident and boast extremely loud,
for often one will find they're nearly out of their minds,
        and the schemes that they endorse are entirely asinine.

So, as the masses mount and the mob seems more convincing,
        never feel compelled by the nonsense they're inventing.

12

Just because it's popular doesn't mean they're correct,
     and one should never invest if the dots don't connect.

Remember, due diligence is always necessary
     to navigate the way that the market's known to vary
or else you might find yourself tied to foolish trends
     and dead center when the bubble bursts in the end.

13

The End

Admirael Delphius Chalk pg. 11
(Based on "Admirael Delphius" of the "Great Tulip Book" c. 1640)

Admirael Van Der Eijck Chalk pg. 12
(Based on "Adirael Van Der Eijck" of the "Tulip Book of Pieter Cos" c. 1637)

Admirael Gouda Chalk pg. 3
(Based on "Admirael Gouda" of the "NEHA Tulip Book" c. 1630)

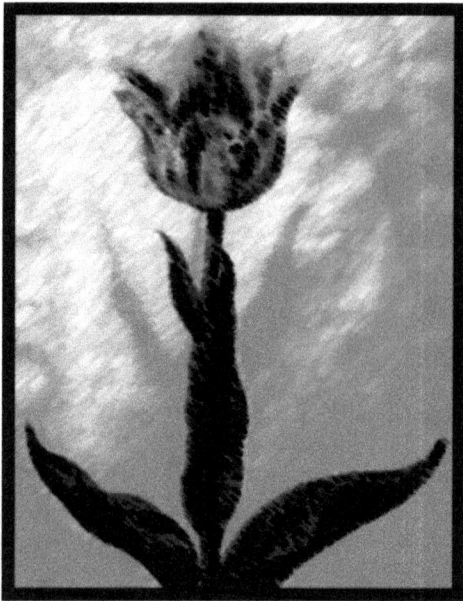

Admirael Tol Chalk pg. 4
(Based on "Admirael Tol" of the "NEHA Tulip Book" c. 1630)

Branson Chalk pg. 9
(Based on "Branson" of the "Great Tulip Book" c. 1640)

De Cleyne Pronckert Chalk pg. 7
(Based on "De Cleyne Pronckert" of the "NEHA Tulip Book" c. 1630)

Fabrij Chalk pg. 2, back cover
(Based on "Fabrij" of the "Great Tulip Book" c. 1640)

De Hoer Chalk pg. 13
(Based on "De Hoer" of the "NEHA Tulip Book" c. 1630)

Latour Chalk pg. 6
(Based on "Latour" of the "Great Tulip Book" c. 1640)

Purper Int Wit Van Jeroen Chalk pg. 5
(Based on "Purper Int Wit Van Jeroen" of the "Great Tulip Book" c. 1640)

Root En Geel Chalk pg. 10
(Based on "Root En Geel" of the "Great Tulip Book" c. 1640)

Semper Augustus Chalk pg. 8
(Based on "Semper Augustus" of the "Great Tulip Book" c. 1640)

Viseroij Chalk pg. 1
(Based on "Viseroij" of the "Tulip Book of Pieter Cos" c. 1637)

www.ingramcontent.com/pod-product-compliance
Lightning Source LLC
Chambersburg PA
CBHW070949210326
41520CB00021B/7123